HEROES
OF
LIBERTY

American values, one story at a time.

HEROES
OF
LIBERTY

John Wayne

MANHOOD AND HONOR

John Wayne

Movies were invented a little more than a hundred years ago. And with them, the first movie stars were born. Over the last century, there have been many stars. But there was never a star quite like John Wayne. He was a legend. And he was a symbol of what a real man should be.

He was also a symbol of what America can be: tough, daring, and self-reliant; big, freedom-loving, and generous.

In John Wayne's book, a real man never looks for trouble, but if trouble comes, he never backs down. America should be that way too.

No one could play a tough guy quite like John Wayne. If you want to look tough, he once said, then talk low, talk slow, and don't say too much.

ACTOR, 1926–1976
HOLLYWOOD, CALIFORNIA

WY

NV

CA

ENROLLED AT THE
UNIVERSITY OF SOUTHERN
CALIFORNIA ON A FOOTBALL
SCHOLARSHIP, 1925
LOS ANGELES, CALIFORNIA

TROJANS

MADE HIS LAST FILM,
THE SHOOTIST – 1976
CARSON CITY, NEVADA

BORN MAY 26, 1907
WINTERSET, IOWA

IA

FIRST LEAD ROLE IN
THE BIG TRAIL, 1930
JACKSON HOLE VALLEY, WYOMING

WENT TO SCHOOL 1916-1925
GLENDALE, CALIFORNIA

His name was not always John Wayne. John Wayne was born Marion Morrison.

He was already big at birth. He weighed 13 pounds, about twice as much as a normal baby. He arrived on May 26, 1907, in the small Iowa city of Winterset.

Ever since he could remember, Marion hated his name. He thought it was a girl's name. Children taunted him about it. "Does your mother also dress you in skirts?" they would say, and they would laugh at him. Marion got into many fights over this. This is one reason why he became so tough.

He was determined to get rid of his name the first chance he got. So he adopted a nickname: Duke. And that's what his friends would call him for the rest of his life.

Life was tough in those days and the Morrisons were poor. But the hardest thing for Duke to bear was not poverty, or even the fights in school.

The hardest thing for this big, strong,
quiet boy to bear was seeing his father fail.

His father, Clyde Morrison, was a very kind man. But he was never any
good at business. He was a pharmacist and owned his own store. But a lot
of times he gave away merchandise for free to people who promised to
pay him back. Not all of them did, and Clyde was sometimes too polite to
remind them. In the end, he went bankrupt and lost his pharmacy.

Duke's mother, Mary—everyone called her Molly—was not as kind. She
would often berate her husband and tell him he was no good.

When she did that, Duke would stay away from the house, wandering outside for hours, just so he didn't have to hear it.

When he was older, Duke would say: "I wish my father knew how much I loved him."

Next, Clyde tried his hand at farming. They moved to a homestead Clyde's father had bought in Southern California.

America had already spread out to reach the Pacific Ocean. California had been admitted into the Union as a state more than a half century before, in 1850. It was no longer the Wild West, but the place was still a wilderness.

The Morrisons lived in a house that was little more than a shack. They had no electricity and no running water. Clyde first tried to grow corn and wheat, two crops that could bring in a lot of money.

But these crops didn't grow well on their farm. The Morrisons lived near the Mojave Desert. Corn and wheat need a lot of water and there just wasn't enough rain. Clyde's plants died, and most of what was left was eaten by jackrabbits.

Clyde was just barely able to feed his family of four—Duke, Duke's little brother Robert, his wife Molly and himself. They got by most days on potatoes and beans.

They did have a horse, though. Her name was Jenny. Duke learned to ride when he was very young. This is why he was so good at it later in his movies. He would wake up at five in the morning to help with the chores around the farm, then he would ride Jenny to school eight miles away, and then eight miles back.

He was just eight years old. Sometimes he would pick up groceries for his family in town and bring them home on his way back from school.

The other kids envied him. Duke was as sure on horseback as they were on foot.

Then, finally it seemed like life would get better. Clyde started growing black-eyed peas, which were better suited to the climate.

Soon they had five acres of beautiful green sprouts. The future seemed bright: when the sprouts grew, they would have a beautiful harvest and could sell the peas for much needed money. So many things needed fixing around the house. Clyde was happy and decided that the family could finally afford a short vacation. They left the farm for a weekend of fun and had a great time.

But when they returned, it was like the sky had fallen on their heads. Jackrabbits had eaten everything! Nothing was left from all of their beautiful green sprouts. They stared at the barren fields in shock.

Clyde walked through the dry fields like a man who had lost his way. There were tears in his eyes. All of the hard work and all of the big hopes now lay in waste under the merciless desert sun.

It didn't take Molly long to start berating her husband again. She told him she knew nothing good would ever come of anything he did.

Duke was too young to support his father. But he never forgot that day.

In the end, the Morrisons gave up the
farm and moved to Glendale, California.
Clyde took up a job at a pharmacy.

For Duke, there was one great thing about Glendale: it had a
movie theater. And it was there that Duke fell in love with the
cinema. He worked a newspaper delivery route and saved every
penny he could in order to buy movie tickets. In the darkness
of the theater, he would forget himself and his family
troubles. He spent hours there, sometimes watching the same
film over and over again. He liked Westerns most of all, and
his favorite star was Tom Mix, who played tough cowboys.

Duke's love for Tom Mix is how he got his nickname. He loved animals, and when he finally got a dog, he named him after the dog that played alongside Tom Mix in his movies: Duke.

Duke the dog loved to hang out at the Glendale firehouse while his owner was in school. So the firemen soon started calling the dog Little Duke, and the boy, who was now big and tall, Big Duke. The name stuck.

The firemen liked them both—the friendly dog and the big, shy, thoughtful boy. They could tell that Big Duke was lonely, so they made sure to show him they cared with a good word or a glass of milk.

Duke got into a lot of fights at school back then. He wouldn't back down when kids laughed at his name. He was a strong boy so he was okay most of the time. But sometimes older and stronger boys would pick on him, and though he could hold his own, he would take a rough beating every now and then.

The firemen would see his bruises when he passed by the firehouse on his way home. He was not the type to complain, but they saw his pain. They saw that he had no one to talk to and they wanted to help him out.

"Hey Duke," a fireman said one day, "why don't you come over to the firehouse, and I'll teach you some boxing, ey? What do you say?"

"Why, I'd sure like that," Duke said.

He loved those brave guys, who risked their own lives to save the lives of strangers.

His newly acquired boxing skills came in handy. Older bullies would soon discover that Duke could give as good as he got. You can bet he never looked for trouble. But he sure didn't back down if it came!

Later, his fans would think of John Wayne as a rough guy. But the truth was that he was also a very good student. He was class president during his senior year of high school and his good grades earned him admission to USC—the University of Southern California. He planned to be a lawyer.

But his family didn't have enough money to pay the tuition. He may have never gone there had he not also been a good athlete.

He qualified for the USC football team—the Trojans. Lucky for him, university football players got scholarships: the university helped them pay for their studies.

So Duke did go to USC, but he never became a lawyer. Instead it was USC that helped make him a movie star, though this wasn't anyone's intention. It all came together by chance. And it all started with Tom Mix. Yes, the same Tom Mix that Duke admired. Because, you see, Mix loved football.

The Trojans' coach had a deal with Tom Mix. They would give him tickets to the best seats at their games, and in exchange, Tom Mix would help the players get summer jobs at film studios.

This is how Duke got his first job as a prop man. The prop man is responsible for getting all the physical objects the actors handle on a film set. If an actor plays a passenger, the prop man gets him a suitcase.

Or if the director wants to shoot a scene with autumn leaves blowing in the wind, and they can't wait for the autumn to shoot it, then a prop man like Duke stands by a huge fan and throws leaves in the air so the fan can blow them past the actors. There are hundreds of such things the prop man needs to take care of: kettles, telephones, pistols, umbrellas, binders, binoculars, or even a cooked Thanksgiving turkey if you have a Thanksgiving dinner scene in the film.

When summer break was over, Duke's job as a prop man was over too. Duke went back to college to study and play for the Trojans. But one day, while surfing, he injured his shoulder. He tried to hide it, but it was no use. He couldn't play football with a bad shoulder. And so he lost his football scholarship and had no money to pay for his studies. He ended up taking a year off from USC and turned his summer job into a full-time job: he became a regular prop man. The idea was to save enough money and go back to college. But it wasn't to be, because fate intervened. One day a famous director named Raoul Walsh saw the big handsome prop man carrying an armchair over his head.

"Hello there, young feller," he said. "How would you like to be in a picture?" (This is what they used to call movies back then).

"Oh, I'd like it right well," said Duke (They used to say "right well" instead of "very much" back then).

"Why don't you let your hair grow for a few weeks and come back to me?" said Walsh. And believe it or not, this is how Duke got his first lead role in a major motion picture. It was called *The Big Trail*.

In *The Big Trail*, Duke plays a trapper named Breck Coleman, who joins a wagon caravan of settlers heading West on the Oregon Trail. He plans to follow the bad guys who have escaped to the Wild West.

What was the Wild West? Why would people risk everything they had to get there? The West back then was a place of boundless opportunities. You could start over and make a new life for yourself. You could buy cheap land and cultivate it. You could get lucky and find gold in the earth. But it was also a place of great risk. War with Native American tribes could break out at any time. Crops could fail, or bad men could harass or even rob you.

And the problem was that there was no one in the wild western frontier to enforce the law. There were no courts yet; there weren't even police. For both heroes and villains, for the bold and the reckless, for the brave and the free, for trailblazers and pioneers, and also for con men and criminals—it was a place of big dreams that could also turn into nightmares.

Naturally, it was a perfect place for movies. Because life in the Wild West could put people to the test and anything could happen there.

In the end, Breck Coleman, the character that Duke played, finds the bad men and makes sure justice is served. Along the way, he meets a girl, and they fall in love. Just like in the movies. Because—of course—it is a movie.

There's one more reason why *The Big Trail* is memorable. It was where Duke got his screen name. The producers didn't like the name Marion Morrison. They also didn't think Duke Morrison sounded like a star's name. So without even asking him, they decided to call him John Wayne.

Duke discovered his new name only when he saw it on the big screen. Imagine that! It's a good thing that he liked his new name, because it stuck. From then on, the whole world would know him as Mr. John Wayne.

John Wayne played many hero roles. It seemed to suit him naturally—his voice, his size, and the way he looked people in the eye. He spoke low, he spoke slow, and he didn't say too much. But when he said something, you knew he meant it. And the bad guys seemed to know this too: if you crossed him, you crossed him at your own peril.

John Wayne starred in many more films. The shy boy, whom kids harassed because of his name, became the most famous of all movie stars!

One of the secrets to his success was that John Wayne stayed true to Duke Morrison. He always acted honorably, to men and to women alike, and he always observed this rule: the characters he played would never shoot anyone in the back. John Wayne behaved just like Duke Morrison believed men should. They should be tough but always fair. Not just when it is easy, but also when it's hard.

In a famous movie called *The Man Who Shot Liberty Valance*, John Wayne's character, Tom Doniphon, protects the innocent from bad-man Liberty Valance's gang of thugs. There is also, of course, the girl he loves. Her name is Hallie.

One day these thugs beat up a young lawyer named Ranse. Hallie treats Ranse's wounds and falls in love with him. This hurts Tom very much, because he dreamed of marrying Hallie one day. But he says nothing.

Ranse is not a coward, and he decides to avenge his honor and challenge Liberty Valance to a gunfight. They face off in a duel. Liberty Valance laughs. He is so good with his gun that he is sure Ranse has no chance. But against all odds, when the last shot is fired, it is bad-man Liberty Valance that falls.

Everyone thinks Ranse shot Liberty Valance and they all consider him a hero.

But it was not Ranse. It was Tom. He knew Ranse couldn't win, and so he shot Liberty Valance from the shadows.

Hallie believes Ranse is the hero and she marries him. Tom loves her so much that he doesn't want to spoil her happiness by telling her the man she married is not the hero that she thinks he is. He keeps it all to himself, even though his own heart is broken.

This was the kind of man Duke loved to play: tough on his enemies, loyal to his friends, a gentleman with women, and deeply committed to those he loves.

One day, when he was already a famous star, Duke went to USC to help raise money for a children's hospital. Walking through the campus of his old university, he saw students protesting against the war in Vietnam. America entered that war to protect South Vietnam from attacks by its neighbor, communist North Vietnam. The students thought America had no business fighting there.

Then a young marine in uniform walked by. The students started shouting at him.

They called him names. They taunted him.

Only then did Duke notice that one of the young marine's sleeves was empty, attached with a pin to his jacket. He had lost his arm in the war, defending South Vietnam. Duke came over to speak with him. "It's alright," the marine said. "I just ignore them." But he was awfully glad to have John Wayne on his side!

Duke's blood was boiling. He walked over to the protesting students and banged his fist on their table.

"How dare you insult this young man!" Duke wanted to know.

"We have no business being in Vietnam!" one student said.

"Well," said Duke, "you can protest against the leaders who sent him there if you want, but you have no business insulting an honorable young man who put his life on the line for other people! You should be ashamed of yourselves."

It was then and there that Duke
decided to make a movie about brave
American men, like that marine who lost
his arm—men fighting to protect the freedom
of a faraway people, as the United States has often done.
The movie was called *The Green Berets*, because marines wear green
beret hats. John Wayne played Colonel Mike Kirby, a marine commander, who
leads his men through the jungles of Vietnam.

A lot of people who believed that America should have never gotten involved
in the war in Vietnam were angry at John Wayne. But he stood by his film
and his firm conviction that America should stand up against the enemies
of freedom. Because when trouble comes, you just don't back down.

John Wayne made movies as long as he could. Three years before his death, he made his last one, *The Shootist*. It's the story of an old man, J.B. Books, who was once a sheriff. No one could use a gun as well as Books could. But now, he is terminally ill. He knows he doesn't have much time left. So he chooses to do battle against three bad men. If he has to go down, he'll go down fighting.

Duke himself was very ill too. The people who worked with him on the film had a creeping bad feeling. Was Duke's life starting to resemble the story of his character too closely? Would John Wayne go down shooting a film, as the character he played goes down shooting his gun?

Duke had beaten lung cancer many years before. But it cost him one lung. He now had only one, and it was infected with pneumonia. They had to stop shooting the film. For a while, there were many whispers around the set. What if he didn't recover? Some even considered finishing the film with someone else who looked like Duke. But John Wayne was no quitter. He finished the film. He played it to the last scene, in which Books dies, while he himself persevered and recovered.

Generations of stars came and went, but there was only one John Wayne and he towered over them all.

Duke retired after *The Shootist* and could finally devote his time to the one thing he loved as much as making movies: spending time with his seven children and many grandchildren. He loved to take them on his yacht where they would fish, chat, laugh, or sometimes just stare in silent wonder at the vast, vast blue ocean.

For the entire world, Duke was the famous, tough, John Wayne. For them, Duke was Daddy and Grandpa—the father and the grandfather who loved to play and joke around.

Duke—John Wayne—passed away in 1979. But his movies will live forever. And with them, the great ideas Duke believed in. Ideas about America's role in protecting freedom around the world, about manhood, and about honor, about what this great country should always aspire to be: a big, tough, generous nation that does not look for trouble, but will never back down if it comes.

7

INTERESTING FACTS ABOUT
John Wayne

JOHN WAYNE MADE MORE
THAN 200 FILMS.

THE BIG TRAIL

THE FIRST MOVIE HE STARRED IN,
THE BIG TRAIL, WAS ACTUALLY
A BOX OFFICE FAILURE.

FOR A FULL DECADE AFTER THE THE BIG TRAIL,
HE WAS NOT CONSIDERED A STAR, AND ONLY
GOT ROLES IN CHEAP B MOVIES.

HE PERSONALLY VISITED AMERICAN TROOPS IN VIETNAM SEVERAL TIMES TO SHOW THEM HIS SUPPORT.

HE ONCE SAID, "I AM GRATEFUL FOR EVERY DAY OF MY LIFE THAT I SPEND IN THE UNITED STATES OF AMERICA."

HE WAS AWARDED THE PRESIDENTIAL MEDAL OF FREEDOM AFTER HIS DEATH.

AFTER HIS DEATH FROM CANCER, HIS CHILDREN FOUNDED THE JOHN WAYNE CANCER FOUNDATION TO HELP FIGHT THE DISEASE.